A Beautiful Creation

•

Text written and selected by
Andrew Killick

All photographs (except page 29)
by **Jennifer Scaife**

The beauty of creation has been spoiled by sin; so how can our relationship with God be restored? We hope this book will be especially helpful to those who, for whatever reason, do not want long verbal explanations.

British Library Cataloguing-in-Publication Data
A catalogue record for this book is available from the British Library.

Published by Destinworld Publishing Ltd.
www.destinworld.com

The world is firmly established; it cannot be moved.

Psalm 93.1

The sea is his, for he made it, and his hands formed the dry land.

Psalm 95.5

The Lord is my light and my salvation – whom shall I fear? The Lord is the stronghold of my life – of whom shall I be afraid?

Psalm 27.1

And why do you worry about clothes? See how the lilies of the field grow. They do not labour or spin. Yet I tell you that not even Solomon in all his splendour was dressed like one of these.

Matthew 6.28-29

All of us, like sheep, have strayed away. We have left God's paths to follow our own. Yet the Lord laid on him the sins of us all.

Isaiah 53.6 NLT

The creation looks forward to the day when it will join God's children in glorious freedom from death and decay.

Romans 8.21 NLT

He will wipe every tear from their eyes. There will be no more death or mourning or crying or pain, for the old order of things has passed away.

Revelation 21.4

I lift up my eyes to the hills – where does my help come from? My help comes from the Lord, the Maker of heaven and earth.

Psalm 121.1-2

Jesus answered, "I am the way and the truth and the life. No-one comes to the Father except through me."

John 14.6

20 ■ Pathway through the woods in Preston Park

"While he was still a long way off, his father saw him and was filled with compassion for him; he ran to his son, threw his arms around him and kissed him. The son said to him, "Father, I have sinned against heaven and against you."

Luke 15.20-21

Jesus stood and said in a loud voice, "If anyone is thirsty, let him come to me and drink."

John 7.37

Call upon me in the day of trouble; I will deliver you, and you will honour me.

Psalm 50.15

"Here I am! I stand at the door and knock. If anyone hears my voice and opens the door, I will come in and eat with him, and he with me."

Revelation 3.20

The Lord is my shepherd...He leads me beside quiet waters.

Psalm 23.1-2

Then I saw a new heaven and a new earth…He who was seated on the throne said, "I am making everything new!"

Revelation 21.1,5

There is so much beauty in the world. And yet the world has been spoiled by sin – human greed and selfishness, ignoring and despising our Creator.

Jesus died on a cross to take the punishment that our sins deserved. This means that the barrier separating us from God can be removed. All we need to do is call on Him, ask for His forgiveness and invite Him into our lives.

To do that will be to start out on a totally new life of joy and peace, serving our Creator God. You could pray the prayer below or use your own words.

"Heavenly Father, forgive me for all the wrong things I have said and done. Thank you that Jesus died in my place and took the punishment I deserved. Please come into my life now. Help me to follow you from now on. Amen."

Index of Pictures

Front cover: Sunrise over fields near Egglescliffe

Rear Cover: Low Force on the River Tees